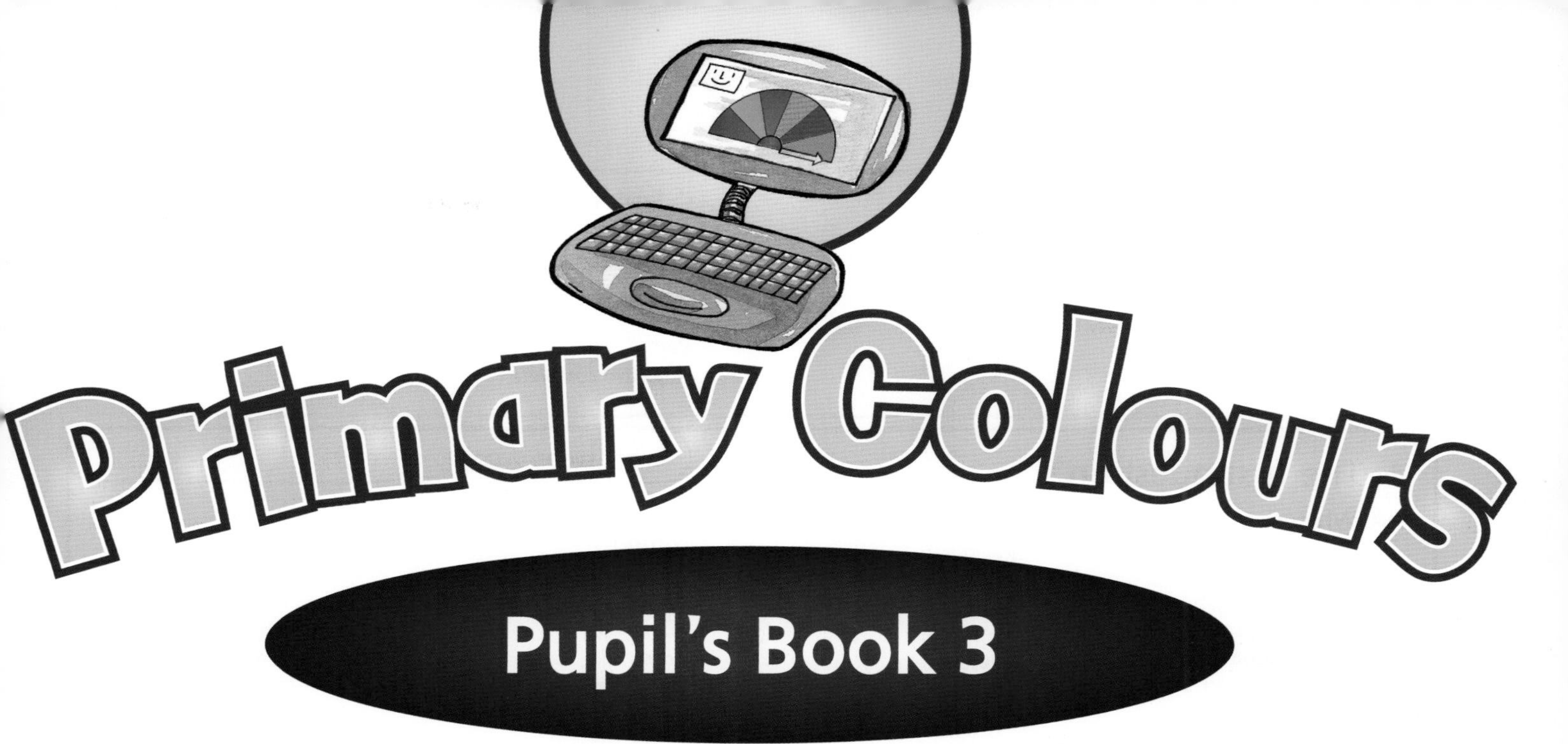

Diana Hicks Andrew Littlejohn

CAMBRIDGE
UNIVERSITY PRESS

Contents

Welcome back!

A Some new friends

1 Listen and follow. What happens to Alex?

2 Follow the lines. What have the children got? Ask and answer.

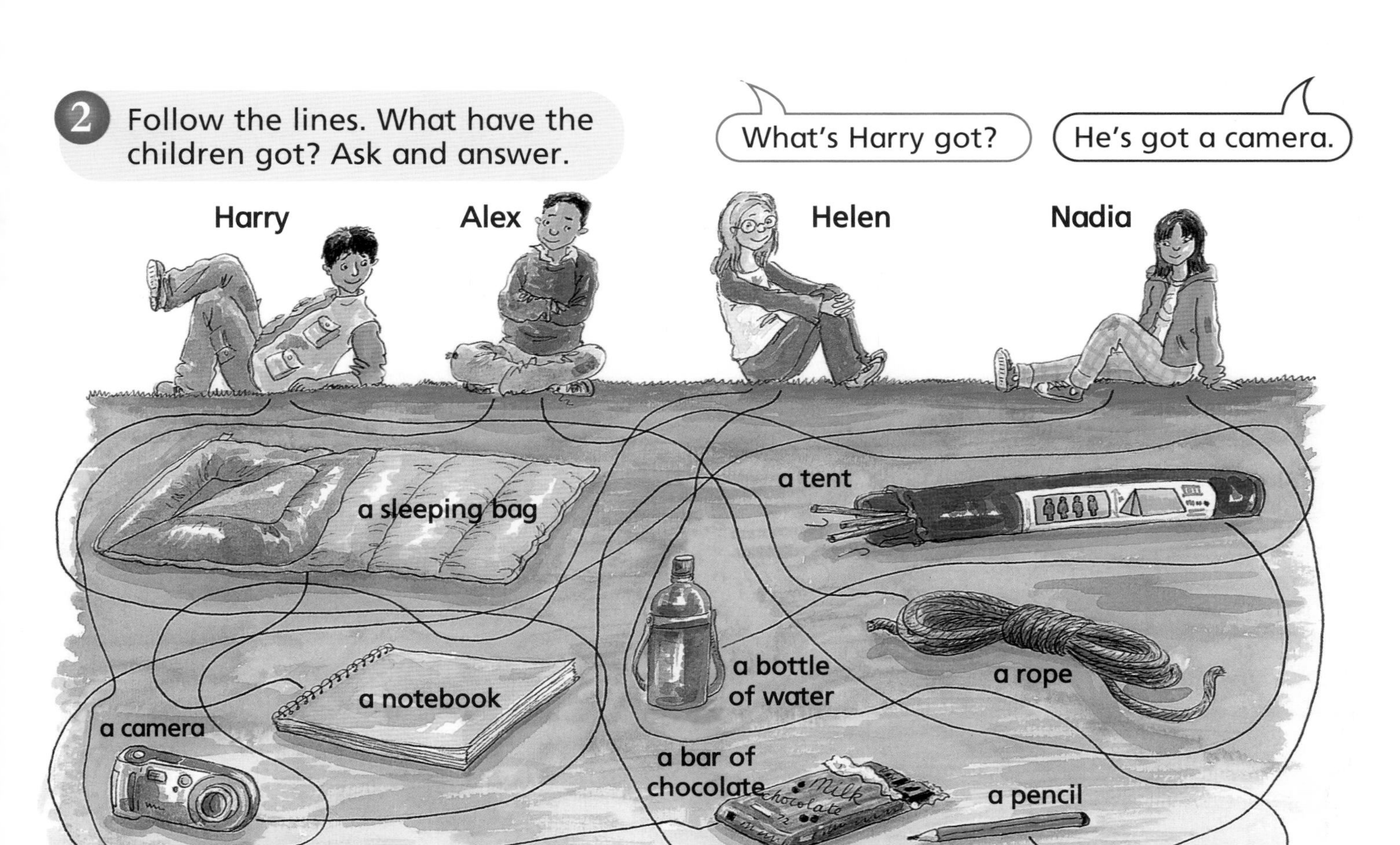

3 Think. What can the children do with the things in Exercise 2? Tell your friend.

They can take photos with a **camera**.

eat write draw ~~take photos~~ sleep drink climb

4 Sing a song. ***When you want some friends.***

When you want some friends to talk to,
Here they are …
When you want some friends to talk to,
Here they are, here they are.

When you want to draw a picture,
Talk to Helen. When you want to.
When you want to draw a picture,
Here they are, here they are.

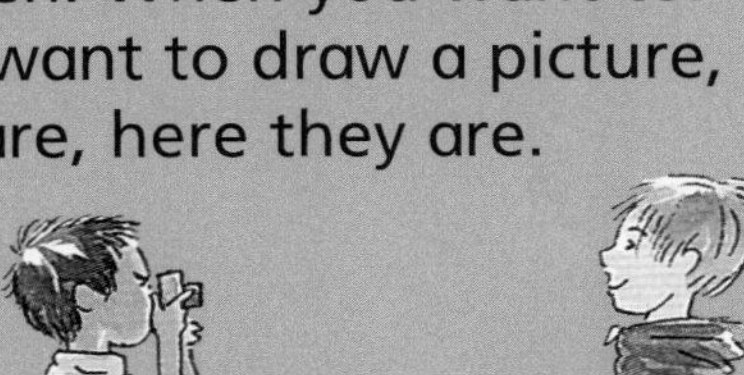

When you want to take a photo,
Talk to Harry …

When you want to fly up high,
Talk to Alex …

When you want to go swimming,
Talk to Nadia. When you want to.
When you want to go swimming,
Here they are, here they are,
Here they are, here they are!

B Hello, Compo!

1 Listen and follow. How can the children go home?

2 Read the sentences and look at the pictures on page 6. Say the names.

1 In picture 2 he's drinking water.
2 In picture 2 he's sitting on Compo.
3 In picture 3 she's eating chocolate.
4 In picture 4 she's looking at a map.
5 In picture 6 they're cleaning their power packs.

Harry.

3a Match the parts to make complete pictures.

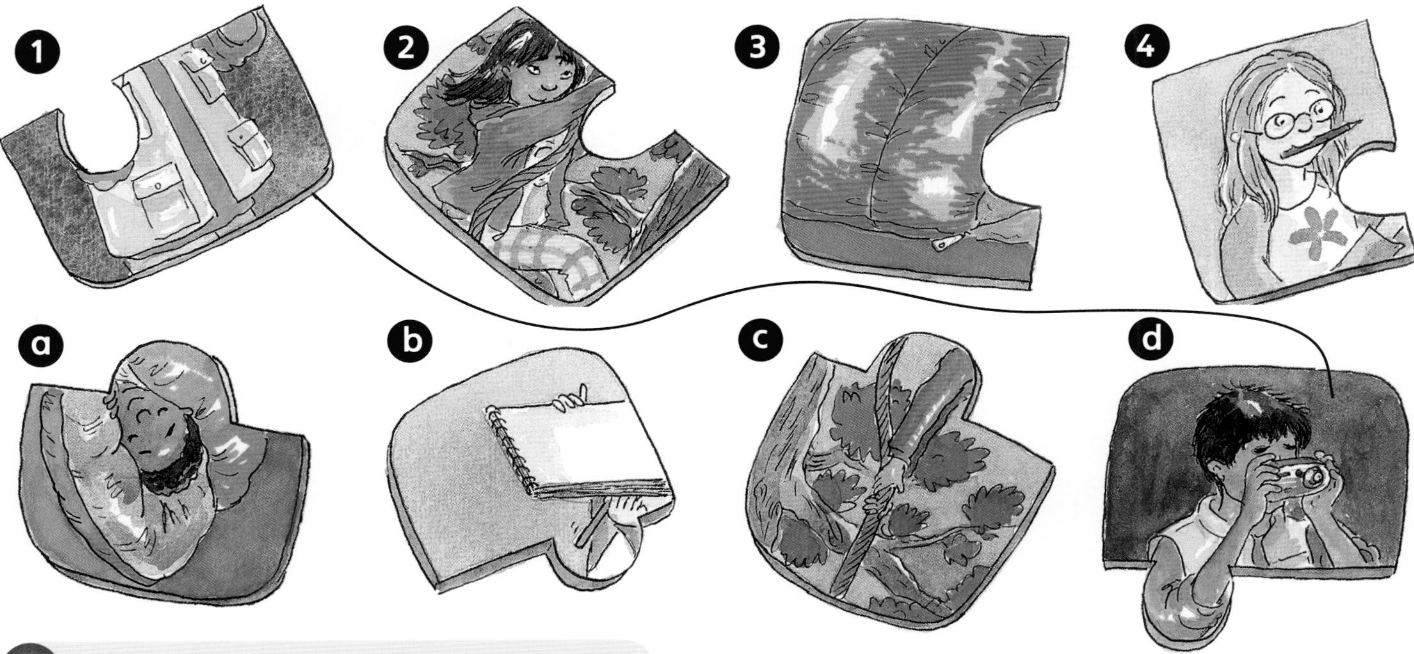

3b Match the parts of the sentences.

1 Harry	A is sleeping in the sleeping bag.
2 Alex	B is drawing a picture with the pencil.
3 Nadia	C is taking a photo with the camera.
4 Helen	D is climbing the tree with the rope.

4 Play a game. Mime an action. Your friend guesses.

1 The first question

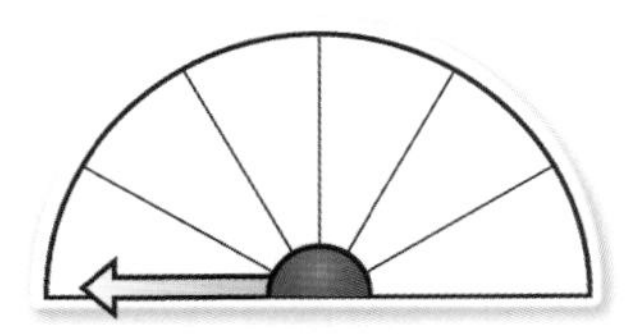

1A Why are there no dinosaurs today?

  Read and listen. What are the children's favourite subjects?

1. 'What questions can we ask Compo?' asked Nadia. 'I don't know,' replied Alex. 'Compo, what questions can we ask you?'

2. 'Look at the screen,' replied Compo. There was a school timetable with six subjects: History, Maths, English, Science, Geography and Social Studies.

3. Compo said, 'You can ask six questions. One from each school subject. Then you can go home.' 'Home! Hooray!' everyone shouted.

4. 'What's your favourite subject at school, Alex?' asked Helen. 'History ... and Maths,' replied Alex. 'History's my favourite subject too,' said Nadia.

5. 'Let's ask about History,' said Nadia. 'OK, umm ... let's ask Compo about the dinosaurs,' said Alex. 'Yes!' replied Harry. 'The dinosaurs were fantastic!'

6. Nadia typed the question, 'Why are there no dinosaurs today?' 'You can travel with your power packs. Go and see the dinosaurs,' Compo replied. 'Wow!' everyone shouted.

  Listen and write the school subject.

	Monday	Tuesday	Wednesday	Thursday	Friday
1	Maths	Science	Geography	Social Studies	....
2	Maths	....	....	....	Science
3	English	Maths	History	History	....
4	Sport	Art	Social Studies	....	Geography
5	Sport	Art	Geography	English	Sport

2b Look and answer.

1 Today is Tuesday: what was lesson 2 yesterday?
2 Today is Wednesday: what were lessons 4 and 5 yesterday?
3 Today is Thursday: what was lesson 3 yesterday?
4 Today is Tuesday: what were lessons 4 and 5 yesterday?
5 Today is Friday: what were lessons 1 and 2 yesterday?

Lesson 2 was Maths.

Lessons 4 and 5 were Art.

3 Ask your friend.

When was your last English lesson?

It was yesterday, lesson 2.

When were your last Science lessons?

They were on Tuesday, lessons 3 and 4.

last English lesson   last Science lessons   last Maths test   last History lesson
last English homework   last Geography homework   last Sport lessons

4 Sing a song. ***We're back at school!***

See page 62 for the words.

1B Back in time!

1 Read and listen. How many different dinosaurs can you see?

1. 'When were the dinosaurs here?' asked Helen. 'About 250 million years ago!' replied Alex. 'Let's go and see them!' 'Hurry up!' shouted Harry.

2. 'This is fantastic!' shouted Alex. 'Where are we going?' asked Nadia. Nadia wasn't very happy about this new adventure.

3. 'Look at the dinosaurs!' shouted Helen. The dinosaurs were all very different. There were enormous dinosaurs and very small dinosaurs.

4. The dinosaurs weren't very quiet and they weren't very nice. 'Look!' said Alex. 'That dinosaur is eating the dinosaur eggs!'

5. The dinosaurs were many different colours. 'Wow!' said Helen, 'Look at all the colours!' 'Oh no!' shouted Alex, 'A volcano! The fire's coming this way!'

6. 'Let's climb this tree!' shouted Alex. The tree wasn't very big. 'No!' shouted Nadia. 'Let's go! It wasn't very nice when the dinosaurs were here!'

2 Are the sentences true or false? Say the correct sentences.

1 Harry was in a tree in picture 2 on page 4.

> No, he wasn't. Helen was in a tree.

2 Harry was in a river in picture 3 on page 4.
3 Alex was in the air in picture 5 on page 4.
4 Compo was under Nadia in picture 2 on page 6.
5 The tree was big in picture 6 on page 10.

3a Look at the picture in Exercise 3b. Answer the questions.

1 How long were the very big dinosaurs?

> The very big dinosaurs were 21 metres long.

2 How long were the very small dinosaurs?
3 What colour were the dinosaurs?
4 Which dinosaurs were plant eaters?
5 Which dinosaurs were meat eaters?

3b Listen and read about dinosaurs. Check your answers to Exercise 3a.

Millions of years ago, there were dinosaurs on Earth. They were here for 165 million years. They were all very different.

There were plant eaters and there were meat eaters. The Brontosaurus, Stegosaurus and Dryosaurus were plant eaters. The Tyrannosaurus Rex and Allosaurus were meat eaters.

The very big Brontosaurus dinosaurs were 21 metres long and the small Dryosaurus dinosaurs were about four metres long. The dinosaurs were many different colours – green, brown, grey and yellow.

Some dinosaurs were very fast and some were very slow. 65 million years ago, there were no more dinosaurs.

1 square = 1 metre

1C www.cambridge.org/compo

1 Sing a song. ***Dinosaurs were big and fast.*** *See page 62 for the words.*

2 Look at the picture for one minute. Cover and ask your friend.

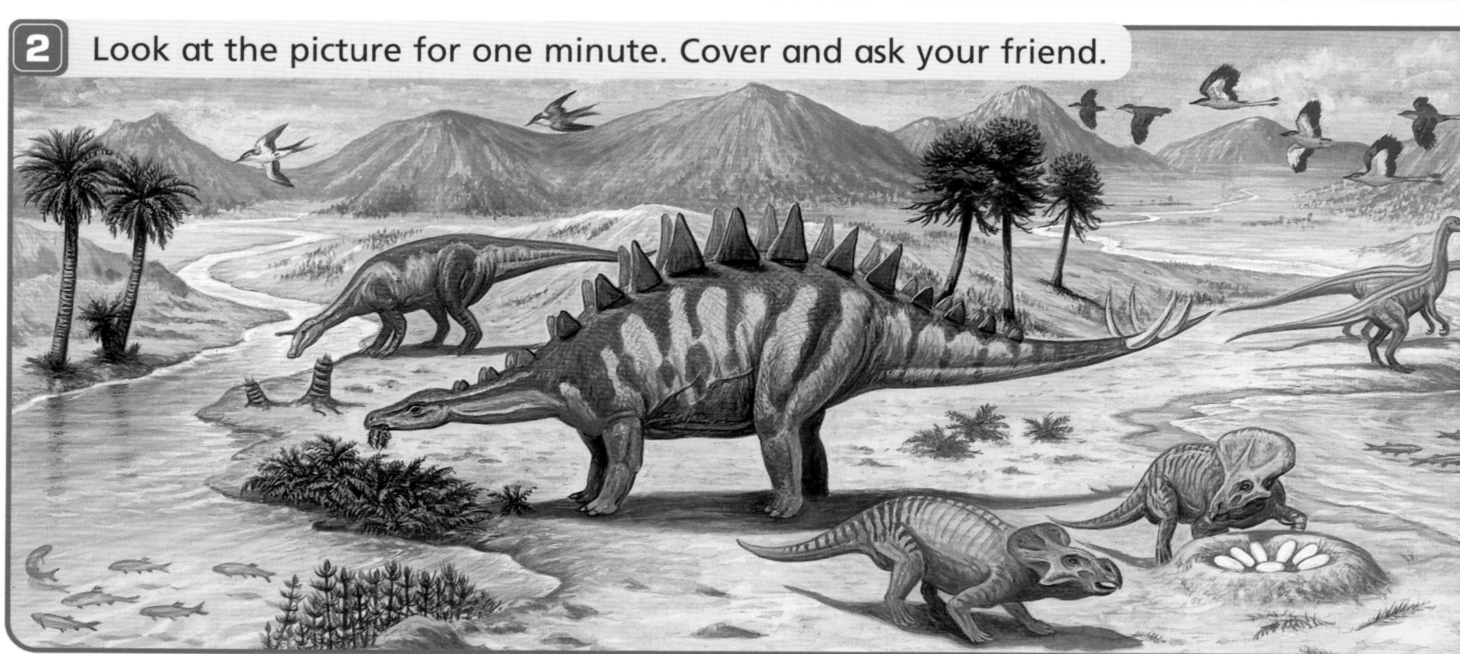

3 Why are there no dinosaurs today? Match the sentences and the pictures.

Back Forward Stop Home Print Mail

~~birds~~ fish mountains eggs
trees lakes rivers dinosaurs

1 There were no more dinosaur eggs. [c]
2 The weather was too hot for the dinosaurs. [ ]
3 There were a lot of volcano explosions and fires on the Earth. [ ]
4 There was a big meteorite and there was no sun or light. [ ]
5 There were no more plants to eat. [ ]
6 There was a big wave from the sea. [ ]

Tell Compo the answers!

Compo: Hello, everyone.
You: *Hello, Compo.*
Compo: Tell me about the dinosaurs.
You: ...
Compo: Great. How big were they?
You: ...
Compo: Good. Were they all the same colour?
You: ...
Compo: Why do people think there are no dinosaurs today?
You: ...
Compo: I see. And what do you think?
You: ...
Compo: Have you got any more ideas?
You: ...
Compo: I see. Very good.

1D Monster in the lake

1 Read and listen. Do you think there was a monster in the lake?

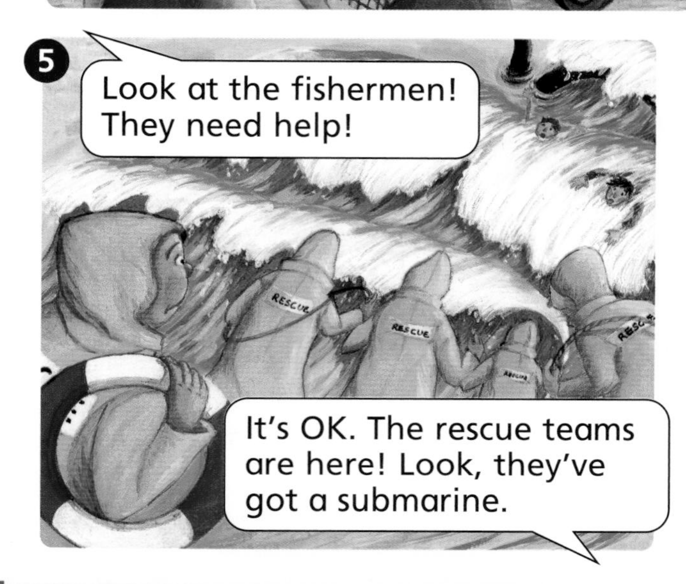

Project work | The monster with two sides

2a Fold a piece of paper in half.

2b Draw one side of a monster on the paper.

2c Give the paper to your friend. Your friend draws the other side of the monster.

2d Write about your monster. Write sentences to answer these questions.

1 Where does it live: on the land, in the air or in the water?
2 What does it eat?
3 How big is it?
4 What colour is it?
5 How fast can it run?

Evaluation

3 Did you enjoy your project? Do you like your monster?

2 The second question

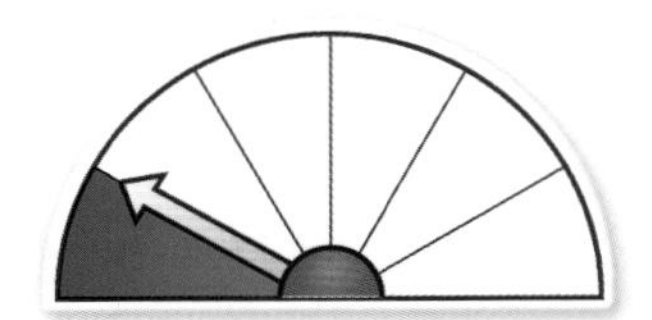

2A Who invented money?

1 Read and listen. How do the children choose the second school subject?

1. The children were happy to be in the 21st century again. 'It was nice to see the dinosaurs, but it was frightening,' said Nadia.

2. 'Let's think about the second question,' said Helen. 'What subjects were on the timetable?' 'History, English, Maths ...' replied Harry. 'Oh no! Not Maths!' said Helen.

3. 'I like Maths,' said Harry. 'Well, I think it's horrible,' said Helen. 'OK, English,' said Nadia. 'I don't know,' replied Alex.

4. 'Let's toss a coin,' said Harry. 'Heads for English and tails for Maths.' 'OK,' said Helen. She looked in her purse for a coin.

5. Helen tossed the coin. It went high in the air. 'Where is it?' asked Helen. 'Here it is!' said Harry. 'It's tails. Maths!' 'Hooray!' shouted Alex.

6. 'What's the question?' asked Nadia. 'Let's ask Compo, "Who invented money?" said Alex. Compo replied, 'Find your power packs. Go and find people with money!'

2a Look at the picture. Ask your friend.

What did Harry do last night?

I think he played football.

- played football
- cooked the dinner
- listened to music
- climbed a tree

2b Listen. Check your answers.

3a Match the two parts of the sentences and the pictures.

Helen's friend, Clare, did lots of things last week. Where did she do these things?

1 On Monday she cleaned the car …
2 On Tuesday she watched videos …
3 On Wednesday she listened to music …
4 On Thursday she played football …
5 On Friday she cooked the dinner …

A in the kitchen. [ ]
B in the garden. [d]
C at home. [ ]
D in her bedroom. [ ]
E in the park. [ ]

a 
b 
c 
d 
e 

3b Look at Exercise 3a for ten seconds. Cover and tell your friend.

Clare played football on Tuesday.

No, she played football on Thursday.

4 Sing a song.
The money song.

See page 62 for the words.

2B Where did they go?

1 Read and listen. What did the woman buy?

1. The children got ready. Nadia packed up the camp, Harry cleaned his power pack, Alex looked for his shoes and Helen filled bottles with water.

2. 'Hurry up!' shouted Harry. The children went up in the air. 'Where are we going?' asked Nadia. 'Compo didn't tell us,' replied Harry.

3. 'Look, everyone!' shouted Nadia. 'There's a big market with a lot of people. Let's go down now.' The children came down and ran to the market. They saw a man. He sold fish.

4. 'Where are we?' asked Nadia. 'In China, 1,200 years ago,' said Compo. A woman walked past. 'That woman bought a fish,' said Harry. 'Did you see her?'

5. 'No, I didn't,' said Helen. 'She had big coins!' 'Did you see her money, Alex?' asked Harry. 'Yes, I did,' replied Alex. 'Did the Chinese people invent money?'

6. 'I don't know,' said Nadia. 'But look at my magic coin!' 'Where did you find it?' asked Helen. 'I found it on the ground,' replied Nadia.

2 Match the questions and the answers.

1 Where did Helen go?
2 Where did the children go?
3 Where did the children come down and run to?
4 What did the market people sell?
5 What did the woman buy?
6 What did the woman have in her hand?
7 Where did Nadia find the coin?

A They sold fruit, bread and fish.
B They went to China.
C She had money in her hand.
D She bought a fish.
E She found it on the ground.
F She went to the river.
G They came down and ran to a market.

3a Listen. Put the pictures in the correct order.

a

b

c

d

e

f

3b What happened next? Write the end of the story.

When Nadia gave her magic coin to the man, he ...

4 Look at the pictures. What did you do last week? Ask and answer.

find

buy

go

go swimming

come

Did you find some money last week?

Yes, I did.

No, I didn't.

2C www.cambridge.org/compo

1 Sing a song. ***Where did you go last night?*** *See page 62 for the words.*

Cinema

Restaurant

2a Think. Are the sentences true or false?

		True	False
1	The Romans invented coins.	☐	☑
2	People made coins 4,000 years ago.	☐	☐
3	The coins were gold and silver.	☐	☐
4	The British first made paper money.	☐	☐
5	People first made paper money 2,000 years ago.	☐	☐

2b Read about the history of money and complete the sentences. Check your answers to Exercise 2a.

Many years ago people didn't have .... They exchanged .... for bread, ... for ...., ... for vegetables, and more.

2,700 years ago people invented money in an old country called Lydia.

The Lydians made .... from gold and silver.

Everyone liked the .... but they were very heavy. About 1,200 years ago, the Chinese people started to make .... money for the first time.

2c Make the false sentences in Exercise 2a true.

The Romans didn't invent coins. The Lydians invented coins.

3 Play a game with a friend.

1 Choose a colour.
2 Ask your friend five questions about the weekend. Use the words in your colour.

buy
go
play
run
paint
make
study
walk
listen
watch

I watched TV at the weekend. Did you watch TV at the weekend?

No, I didn't. I played computer games. Did you play computer games?

Tell Compo the answers!

Compo: Hello, everyone.
You: *Hello, Compo.*
Compo: Where did you find the answer?
You: ...
Compo: And who invented coins?
You: ...
Compo: Where did they have paper money for the first time?
You: ...
Compo: When did they have paper money for the first time?
You: ...
Compo: Excellent. What did people do before they had coins?
You: ...
Compo: I see. Do you think that's a good idea?
You: ...
Compo: Very good. You answered your second question very well!

2D Earning money in the USA

1 Did you do any jobs last week? Ask your friend.

What jobs did you do last week?

2a  Listen. Think. Choose the correct pictures.

Vicki's mum gives her $5 pocket money a week .
How much money did Vicki have at the end of the week?

At the end of the week Vicki had $.................. .

2b Think. The next day Vicki bought three things and came home with no money. What did she buy?

Project work | Class survey

What did you buy last week?

3a Work with a friend. You need Cut-out 1. Write questions.

fizzy drinks | cinema tickets | books

comics | CDs | clothes

computer games | sweets | chocolate

3b Ask your friends.

3c Make a bar chart. You need Cut-out 2.

Evaluation

4 Were you happy with your chart? Would you do it the same next time?

Revision

1a You need Cut-out 3. Write a word in the yellow bricks in each row.

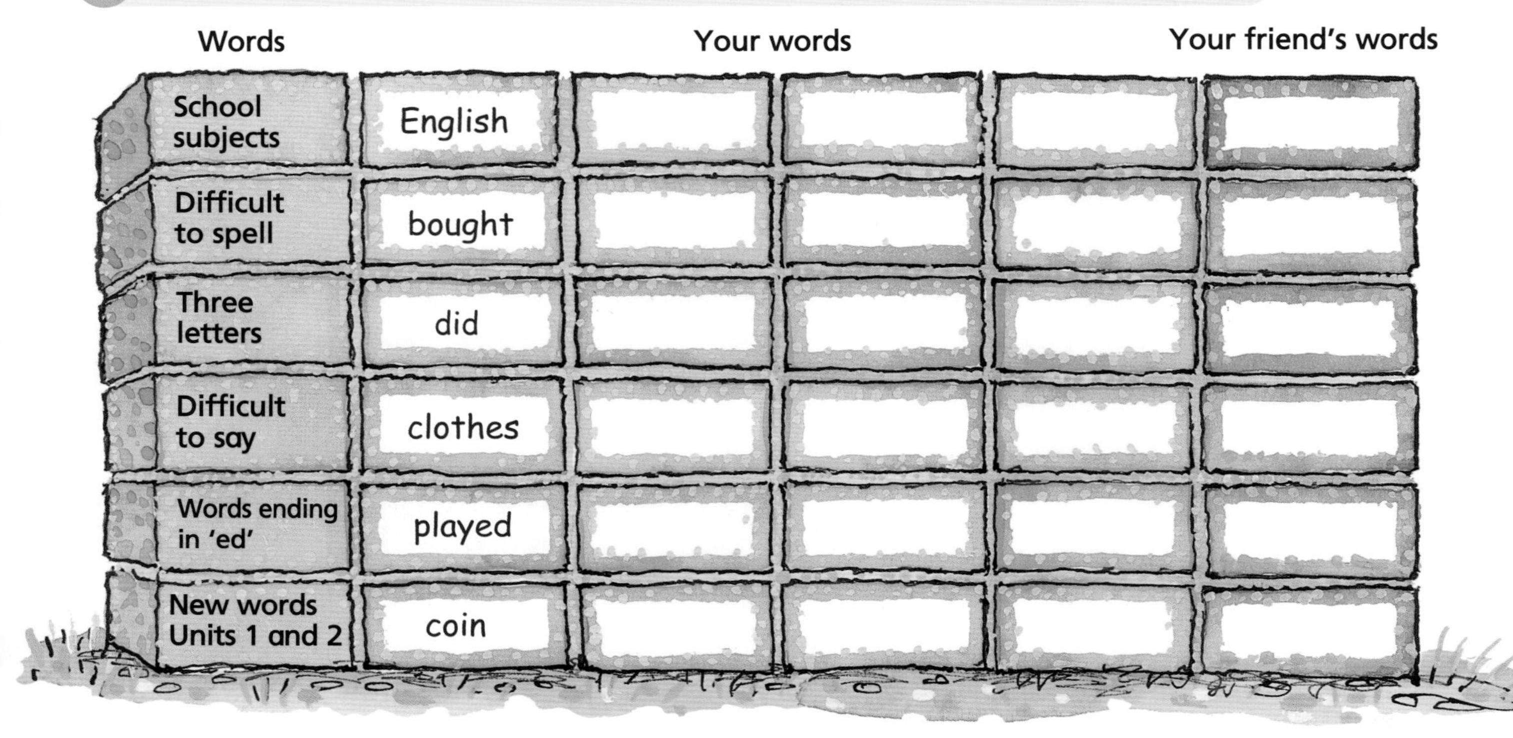

1b Tell your friend your words. Write different words from your friend in the red bricks in Exercise 1a.

2 Look at the calendar. Write a letter to Paul.

Dear Paul,

My family did different things last week. On Monday Dad bought a new computer ...

Monday	2pm - Dad buy a new computer
Tuesday	5pm - David: football match
Wednesday	8pm - Lucy: basketball practice
Thursday	7pm - Mum: Spanish lesson
Friday	6pm - David: clean the car
Saturday	2pm - Picnic with friends
Sunday	

3a Play a game with your friend.

1 Write the numbers 1–9 on pieces of paper.
2 Turn them over.
3 Take a piece of paper.
4 Find the question and your friend answers.

1 Where did the children go first?	F Because they saw a volcano.	9 Where did people first invent coins?
B About 250 million years ago.	6 When did dinosaurs start to live on Earth?	E Tyrannosaurus Rex and Allosaurus were meat eaters.
7 When did people first invent paper money?	D There were no more dinosaurs about 65 million years ago.	3 What subject did the children ask about first?
A In an old country called Lydia.	2 Why did the children run away from the dinosaurs?	C She found a magic coin.
4 What did Nadia find at the market?	I They asked about History first.	8 Which dinosaurs were meat eaters?
G They went to see the dinosaurs first.	5 When were there no more dinosaurs?	H They first invented paper money about 1,200 years ago.

3b Listen and check your answers.

4 Ask your friend more questions about Units 1 and 2.

What did Vicki buy?

She bought …

3 The third question

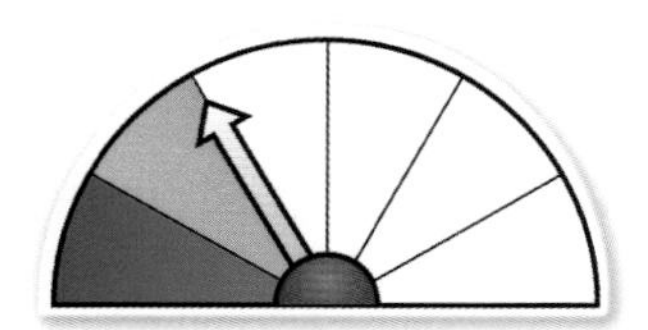

3A Is there a yeti?

  Read and listen. Who liked the yeti story more than the space story?

1. 'It's hot,' said Nadia. 'Yes, let's think of a third question and go to a colder place,' said Harry. They looked at the timetable again.

2. 'I like English,' said Helen. 'But it's more difficult than Science,' replied Harry. 'Let's toss a coin again. Heads for English. Tails for Science,' said Nadia.

3. 'Heads! English!' shouted Helen. 'Let's ask about the stories Mrs Martin told,' said Nadia. 'Yes, do you remember the story about the space people?' asked Alex.

4. 'Yes, but I preferred the story about the yeti. It was more interesting,' said Harry. 'Yes, that was more exciting than the space story,' said Nadia.

5. 'OK, let's ask about the yeti,' said Alex. 'I remember the story. The yeti has got very big feet – bigger than yours, Alex!' laughed Nadia.

6. Harry typed the question, 'Is there a yeti?' 'Take your power packs. Fly to the mountains,' said Compo. 'Hooray! Let's find the yeti!' shouted Harry.

2 Write the names.

It's very cold in the mountains. Compo gives the children new clothes.

Harry's boots are smaller than Helen's.

Alex's sweater is bigger than Harry's.

Alex's trousers are longer than Nadia's.

Helen's scarf is shorter than Nadia's.

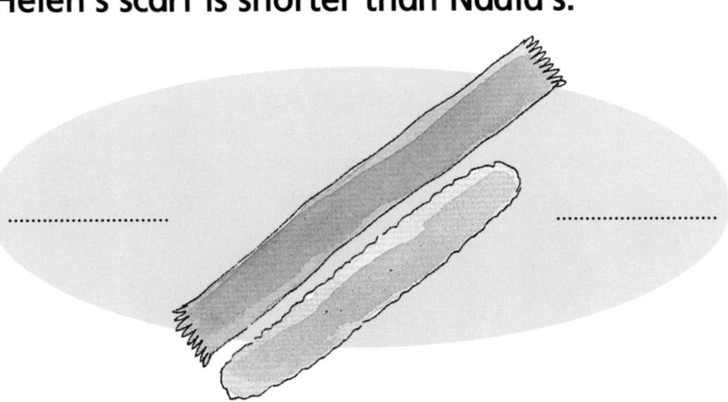

3a These words have got three syllables. Listen. Say the sentences.

1 **dif – fi – cult**
1 2 3

2 **in – terest – ing**
1 2 3

3 **ex – cit – ing**
1 2 3

3b Say the words. Count the syllables and write 1, 2 or 3. Listen and check.

sunny	2	enormous		quiet	
beautiful		crazy		delicious	
warm		important		amazing	

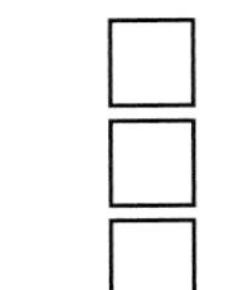

  Sing a song. ***The syllable song.***

See page 63 for the words.

3B The worst day

1 Read and listen. What happened to Harry's camera?

1. It was colder in the mountains than in China. 'Where can we stop?' asked Helen. 'Go to the highest mountain', Compo said.

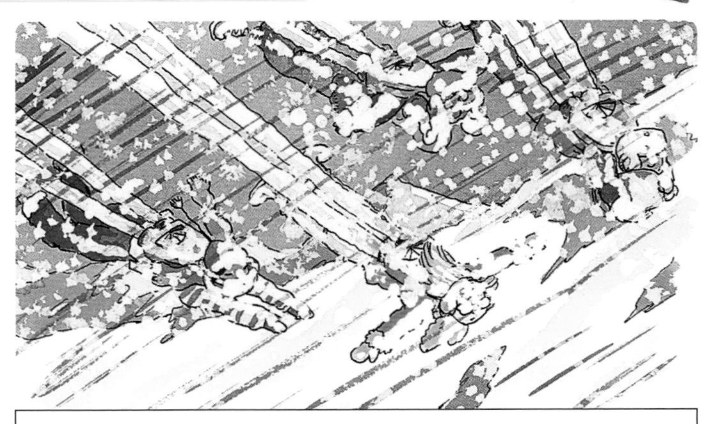

2. The children went higher and higher. It was colder and colder. 'Brrr! This is the coldest place in the world!' said Alex.

3. 'We're here!' said Harry. 'Wow!' said Helen. 'This is the most beautiful place in the world.' A man came and said, 'Come and eat with me.'

4. 'Thank you for the best meal for a long time,' said Harry. 'Tomorrow we can look for the yeti,' said the man, 'but it's very dangerous.'

5. The next morning they went to the mountains. Suddenly the man said, 'Look!' They saw the biggest footprint in the world!

6. Harry found the camera but his hands were very cold and he dropped it. 'Oh no!' shouted Harry. 'This is the worst day of the journey!'

2 Think. Look at the information about the UK and write the answers.

1 The biggest city is London.	Manchester 3,000,000 people	Liverpool 2,500,000 people	London 8,000,000 people
2 The hottest month is	July 21°C	August 19°C	September 15°C
3 The coldest month is	November 4°C	December 2°C	January 0°C
4 The highest mountain is	Mount Snowdon 1,085 metres	Ben Nevis 1,344 metres	Scafell Pike 978 metres
5 The most dangerous animal is	a snake	a fox	a rabbit
6 The oldest place is	Buckingham Palace 1702	The Tower of London 1078	The London Eye 1999

3 Find out about your country.

1 The biggest city is ....
2 The hottest month is ....
3 The coldest month is ....
4 The highest mountain is ....
5 The most dangerous animal is ....
6 The oldest place is ....
7 The best football team is ....

www.cambridge.org/compo

1 Sing a song. ***Monsters! Monsters! Monsters!***

See page 63 for the words.

2 Read about yetis. Write D for Dean and E for encyclopaedia next to the sentences.

1. The yeti is shorter than two metres. [E]
2. The yeti lives in large groups. [ ]
3. The yeti eats meat. [ ]
4. The yeti is yellow. [ ]
5. The yeti sleeps in the cold weather. [ ]
6. The yeti lives outside. [ ]
7. The yeti comes out when it is dark. [ ]
8. The yeti lives longer than people. [ ]

Dean's Story

Dean climbs mountains. He went to the Himalayas a few years ago and saw the yeti. He took photos. He said, 'The yeti is taller than me – about 2.40 metres tall. It is the tallest animal in the mountains. It lives in the biggest cave in the mountains with about 20 yetis. It sleeps all day and eats at night. It eats small animals. It is black. I think they live for about 130 years.'

3 Look at the pictures. Choose one monster and tell your friend. Your friend guesses.

It's not the tallest monster.
It's smaller than monster 3.
It's got the longest hair.

Monster 1!

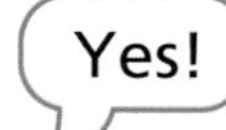

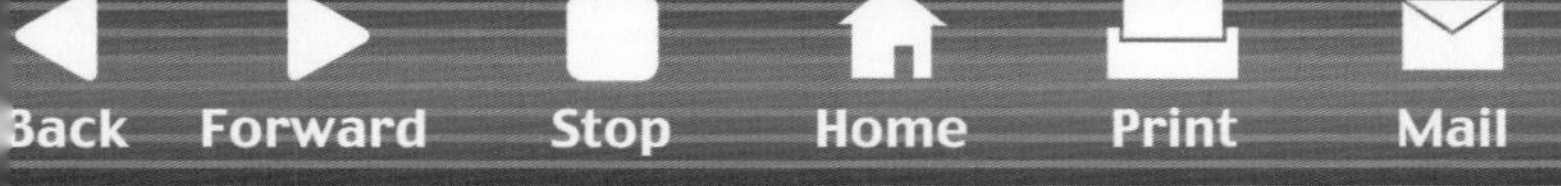

Encyclopaedia

There are many stories about yetis. This story is from the mountain people. Yetis sleep in the three coldest months of the winter. They eat fruit in the summer. They are about 1.60 metres tall – they are taller than the tallest man in the village. They are yellow or yellow-brown. They run very fast – they are the fastest animal in the mountains. They live in trees. They live for about 50 years. They live alone.

Tell Compo the answers!

Compo: Hello, everyone.
You: *Hello, Compo.*
Compo: Do you know about yetis now?
You: ...
Compo: Great. Can you describe a yeti?
You: ...
Compo: Good. Where can you find yetis?
You: ...
Compo: What do you think they eat?
You: ...
Compo: I see. And have people got photos of yetis?
You: ...
Compo: Good. How big do you think they are?
You: ...
Compo: And what do you think now? Do you believe in yetis?
You: ...

3D Coyote girl

1 Read and listen. Which country do you think this story comes from?

1 Once upon a time there were two friends. Blue Maiden was good and Yellow Maiden was horrible.

2 Yellow Maiden went to her house.

Blue Maiden isn't my friend. I can play a trick on her.

3 Yellow Maiden went to Blue Maiden's house.

Let's be friends. Catch!

What a beautiful cloth! Thank you.

4 Blue Maiden caught the magic cloth and quickly fell asleep. Yellow Maiden ran to her house.

Yes! My trick worked.

5 Blue Maiden slept. Two men found Blue Maiden.

Look at this coyote. It can cry.

Let's take it to Grandmother.

6 The two men took the Coyote girl to their grandmother. Coyote girl woke up.

You are a Coyote girl.

Please help me.

7 The grandmother put the Coyote girl into a pot on the fire with some magic plants. Suddenly there was Blue Maiden.

You're OK now. Take this magic cup.

Oh, thank you!

8 Blue Maiden went to see Yellow Maiden. They went to get some water.

Give me that cup. I want to drink from it!

9 Yellow Maiden drank from the cup. Suddenly she turned into a snake!

Project work A chain story

2a Write some more examples of kind and unkind things. Talk about them in class.

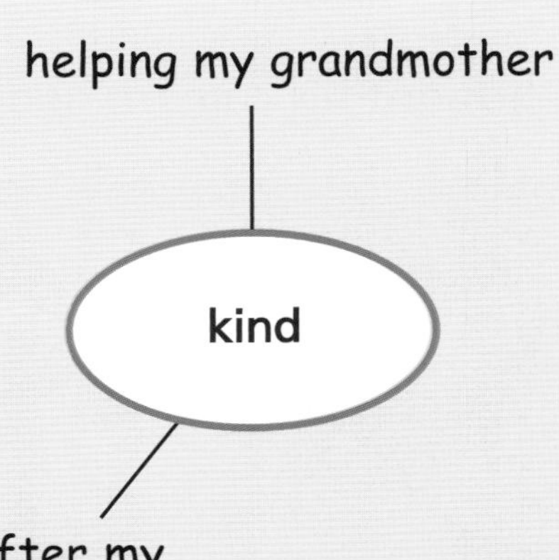

helping my grandmother

kind

looking after my little brother

not talking to a new student

unkind

not looking after my pets

2b Write the first sentence of a story. Give it to your friend.

2c Read the sentence. Write the next sentence. Pass the paper to your next friend.

2d Write a sentence. Pass the paper to your next friend. Do this eight more times.

2e Correct the story and write it again. Draw a picture.

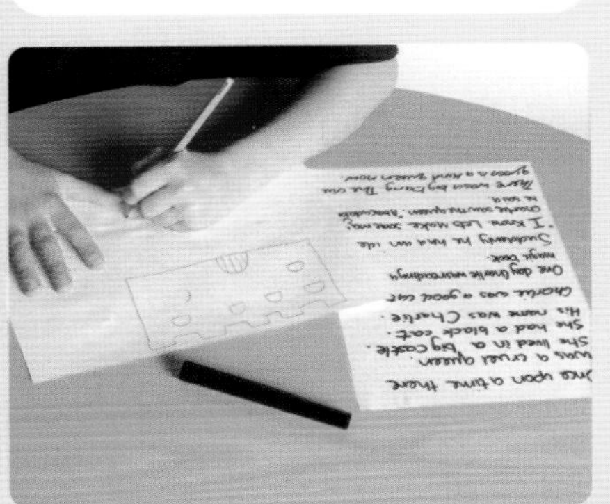

Evaluation

3 Did you prefer writing your sentence or reading the other sentences? Did you like correcting the story at the end? Do you like your story?

4 The fourth question

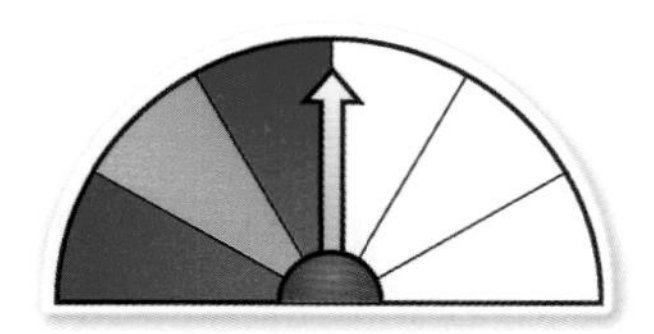

4A Does everyone eat the same food?

1 Read and listen. Why do you think Harry has got his camera again?

1. The children sat in the mountains. 'Do you think there is a yeti, Nadia?' asked Alex. 'Yes, I do now,' replied Nadia ... and she looked at the camera.

2. 'I'm hungry,' said Helen. 'Let's eat. Then we can think about the fourth question.' 'OK,' said Harry. 'Have we got any food?'

3. 'Here's some bread and cheese but I haven't got any fruit,' said Nadia. 'Have you got any chocolate, Alex?' asked Harry. 'No, I haven't. Sorry,' replied Alex.

4. The children ate their small lunch. 'Now, the fourth question,' said Harry. They looked at the timetable. 'Let's ask about Geography,' said Alex. 'OK,' replied Harry.

5. The children walked and saw people. They cooked different food on fires. Suddenly Nadia shouted, 'I know! Let's ask, "What food do people eat in different countries?" '

6. Harry typed the question, 'Does everyone eat the same food?' Compo said, 'Find your power packs and fly to a big city.' Everyone shouted, 'Hooray!'

2 The children go to the supermarket. Match three words to each bag.

1 2 3 4

apples	eggs
bananas	biscuits
spaghetti	yoghurt
bread	cheese
chocolate	water
meat	a pizza

3 Work with your friend. Put three things in your basket. Ask and answer.

Have you got any oranges?

Yes, I have. / No, I haven't.

sweets
spaghetti
tomatoes
rice
oranges
crisps
fizzy drinks
milk

4a Write Q (question), P (positive) and N (negative) next to these sentences.

1 Have we got *any* food? Q

2 There's *some* bread here. ☐

3 And we've got *some* cheese. ☐

4 We haven't got *any* fruit. ☐

5 Have you got *any* chocolate? ☐

6 There isn't *any* here. ☐

4b Can you see a pattern? Match the word and the type of sentence.

Question: any .... Positive: .... Negative: ....

5 Sing a song. ***The picnic song.***

See page 63 for the words.

4B I'm hungry

1 Read and listen. Which restaurant does Nadia go to?

1. 'I'm hungry,' said Helen. 'Look! Lots of restaurants! American, Chinese, Indian and Italian,' said Harry. 'Let's go to different restaurants,' said Nadia.

2. 'I want to eat some Chinese food,' said Helen. 'Some Indian food for me,' said Harry. 'And Italian for me,' said Alex. 'Bye!'

3. Harry went into the Indian restaurant and looked at the menu. 'What would you like to eat?' asked the waiter. 'Can I have some vegetable curry and rice, please?' replied Harry.

4. Alex went to the Italian restaurant. 'Can I have a cheese and tomato pizza, please?' 'What would you like to drink?' asked the waiter. 'Some orange juice, please.'

5. In the Chinese restaurant, Helen said, 'Can I have some noodles, please?' 'Sorry, we haven't got any noodles,' the waitress said. 'Can I have some spring rolls, please?' said Helen.

6. Nadia went into the last restaurant. She looked at the menu. 'What would you like to eat?' asked the waitress. 'Hmm …' Nadia said.

2 Look at the restaurants and the meals. Where can you eat these meals? Tell your friend.

I think you can eat vegetable curry and rice in the Indian restaurant.

3 What did Nadia eat and drink? Look at the menu and listen.

4 Think. Look for a pattern. Tell your friend.

4C www.cambridge.org/compo

1 Sing a song. ***Food, food, wonderful food!***

See page 63 for the words.

2a Listen and write the numbers.

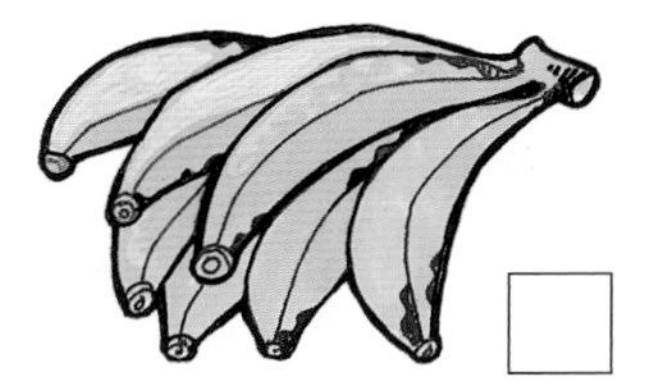

bananas

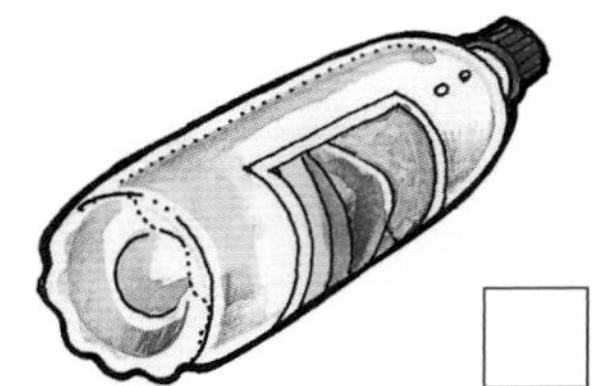

litre of water

bars of chocolate

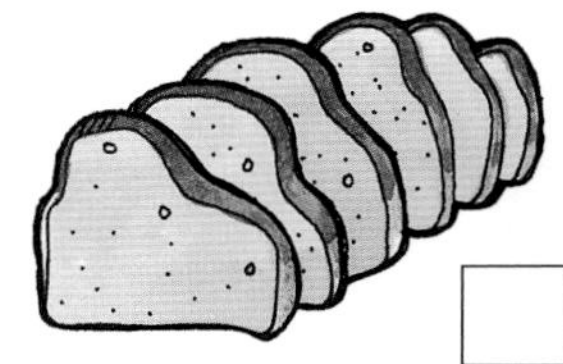

slices of bread

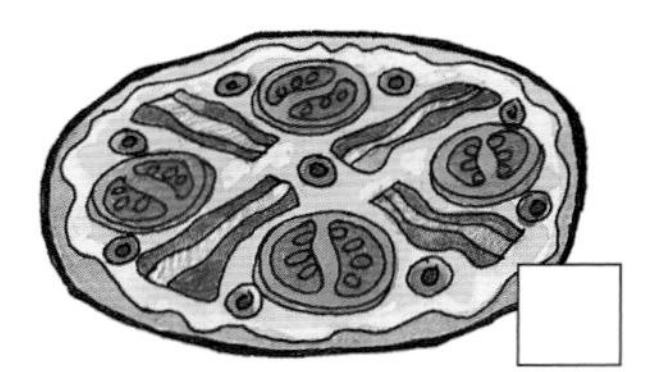

pizza

cans of fizzy drink

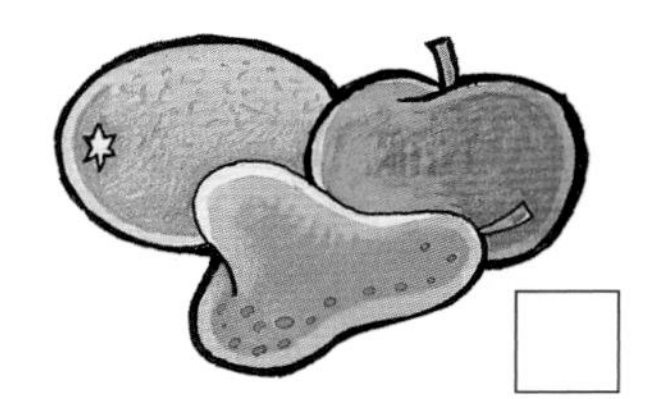

fruit

bowls of rice

3 Look at the menu. Some meals are in the wrong place. Draw lines to the correct places.

INTERNATIONAL INTERACTIVE CAFÉ

menu

Italian
Italian
Chinese
Indian
Italian
American
American
American

2b Ask and answer.

How many bananas do you eat every day?

One.

How much water do you drink every day?

One litre.

bananas water chocolate bread
pizza fizzy drinks fruit rice

4 Work with two friends. One is the waiter and two are customers.

Hello, what would you like?

I'd like some curry, please.

Would you like any …?

Anything else?

Can I have a pizza, please?

Sorry, we haven't got any …

Anything to drink?

Some water, please.

Tell Compo the answers!

Compo: Hello, everyone.
You: Hello, Compo.
Compo: What do you know about food from different countries?
You: …
Compo: Great. What do people eat in China?
You: …
Compo: Good. And what do people eat in India?
You: …
Compo: OK. What do people eat in Italy?
You: …
Compo: I see. Do you eat food from other countries?
You: …
Compo: What is your favourite food?
You: …
Compo: Mmm. I like that too.

4D What do they eat in Australia?

1 Look at the pictures of the restaurants. You are in Sydney. Which restaurant do you go in? Why?

2 Match the pictures and the texts.

1 Most Australian cities are by the sea. Many Australians like to swim or fish in the sea. Then they meet together in the evening for a barbecue in the park or at home. They cook meat and fish on the barbecue. ☐

2 For two hundred years, Australians ate British food. Now, there are restaurants from all over the world in Australia. Chinese restaurants came first because many Chinese people arrived between 1850–1870. They came to work in the gold mines. ☐

3 In Queensland the farmers grow a lot of fruit – bananas, melons, tomatoes, grapes and sugar cane. Trains and lorries take the fruit to the cities in the south. There are many different types of fruit in the shops. ☐

4 There are crocodiles in the rivers and in the sea. Crocodile 'farmers' catch and kill them and sell the crocodile meat to restaurants. Some people say that it is wrong to kill crocodiles to eat. ☐

a

b

c

d

Project work — Design a menu for your restaurant

3a Work with a friend. What do you eat and drink in your country? Use your dictionaries.

Breakfast	Lunch	Dinner	Celebrations

3b Make a menu of your country's food. Give your restaurant a name.

3c Use the menu and prepare a role play in your restaurant.

Evaluation

4 Did you like working with different friends? What was easy? What was difficult?

Revision

1a You need Cut-out 4. Write a word in the red bricks in each row.

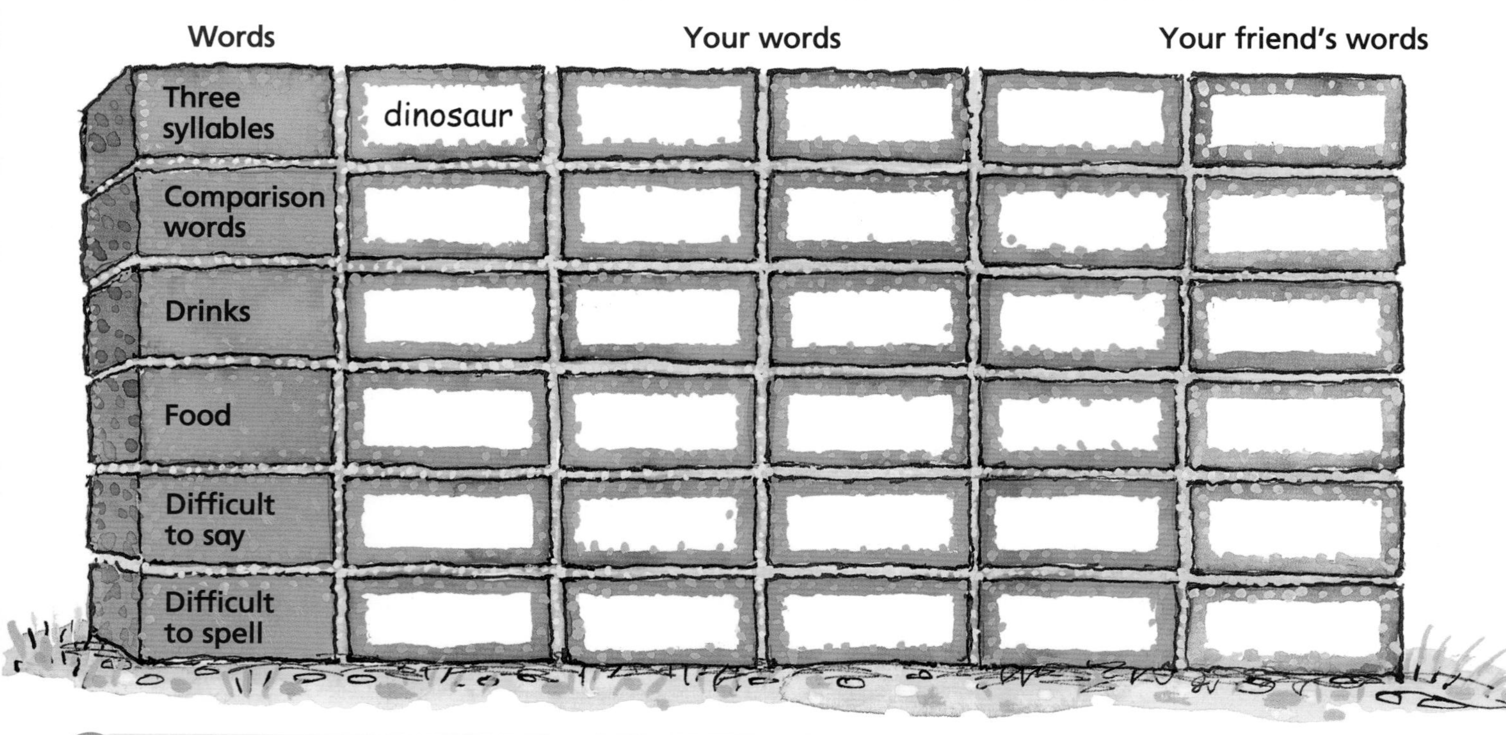

1b Tell your friend your words. Write different words from your friend in the blue bricks in Exercise 1a.

2 Look at the picture for 20 seconds. Cover and ask your friend.

How many eggs are there in the fridge?

There are nine eggs in the fridge.

eggs   fizzy drinks   apples
cakes   bananas   sandwiches

How much meat is there in the fridge?

There isn't any meat in the fridge.

meat   cheese   milk
chocolate   pizza   orange juice

3 Choose three words. Find two things in the classroom. Ask your friend.

tall long big small short

What is bigger than my pen? It begins with 'd'.

Is it a door?

No.

Is it a desk?

Yes.

4 Match three columns. Make sentences.

Mount Everest is higher than Mount Kenya.

1 Mount Everest 8,848 metres; Mount Kenya 6,715 metres	Mount Everest	big	a rabbit
2 River Amazon 6,518 kilometres; River Nile 6,671 kilometres	The River Nile	cold	Mount Kenya
3 Earth; Mars	Earth	dangerous	August
4	The yeti	tall	Mars
5	A crocodile	long	a man
6 APRIL 13°C; AUGUST 20°C	April	high	the River Amazon

5 The fifth question

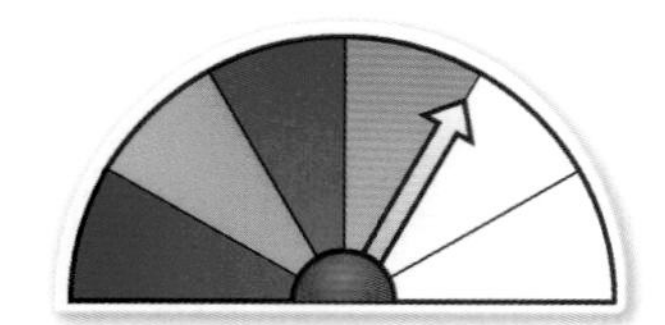

5A How can we clean the world?

  Read and listen. What did the children do in Social Studies?

1. The children bought some food and had a picnic. 'Two more questions and then we can go home!' said Nadia.

2. 'Are we going to ask about Science or Social Studies?' asked Harry. 'What did we do in Social Studies?' asked Helen. 'We did road safety …'

3. '… and dirty air, smoke from cars, pollution.' 'And hygiene,' said Alex. 'We should wash our hands before meals.' Everyone's hands were very dirty. The children laughed.

4. Some people finished their picnic and walked to the road. 'Look! People should take their rubbish home or put it in the bin. They shouldn't leave it there,' said Harry.

5. 'Come on. Let's put everything in the recycling bins,' said Harry. 'I know!' shouted Alex. 'Let's ask Compo how we can clean the world.' 'Good idea!' shouted everyone.

6. Harry asked Compo, 'How can we clean the world?' Compo replied, 'Go and see. Are you ready?' 'Yes! Come on,' said Harry. 'Let's go!'

2 Look at the poster and read the sentences.

3 Look at the pictures. What's wrong?

He shouldn't drive an old car. He should go by bus.

4 Sing a song. ***Rubbish! Rubbish! Rubbish!***

See page 64 for the words.

5B What did we do?

1 Read and listen. What are the differences between the city of the past and the city of the future?

1. The children flew away. Suddenly Compo said, 'Helen and Nadia, you are going to go back in time. Alex and Harry, you are going to go into the future.'

2. The children separated. 'Where are we going?' asked Nadia. 'We're going to fly to London to the year 1900.' 'Wow!' replied Nadia.

3. The girls arrived in London. 'The streets were dirty in 1900,' said Helen. 'Yes, and there was a lot of smoke,' said Nadia.

4. The boys arrived in a city in 2110. 'It's clean!' said Alex. 'Look! People put everything in different bins. They're going to recycle their rubbish,' said Harry.

5. Helen and Nadia walked round London. There was a bad smell and rubbish everywhere. 'I don't like it here,' said Helen. 'Let's go back to the 21st century.'

6. 'Do you like it here?' asked Harry. 'Yes, I like all the machines,' replied Alex. 'But I think we should go and find the girls now,' said Harry.

2 Look at the picture. What isn't the person going to do now? What aren't the people going to do now? Tell your friend. Your friend guesses.

This person isn't going to play tennis.
This person isn't going to play football.

Number four. She's going to ride her bike.

Yes!

3 Listen and write the numbers.

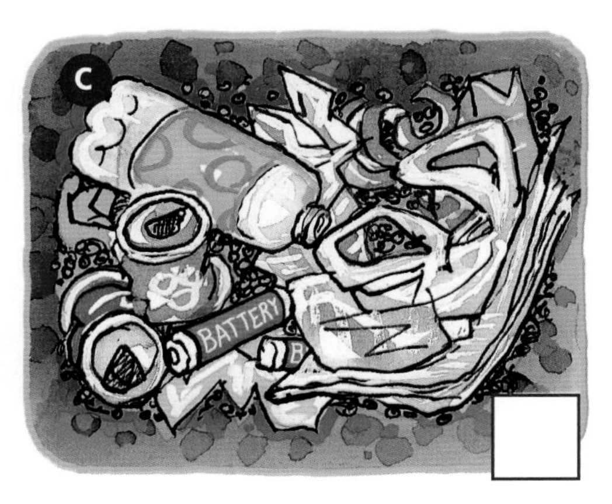

5C www.cambridge.org/compo

1 Listen and read about 'Visionscape'. Label the picture.

2 Complete the sentences.

1 When you finish a can of fizzy drink *you should put it in the recycling bin.* ....
2 When you write a letter ....
3 When you go shopping ....
4 When you finish reading a comic ....

3 Sing a song. ***Reduce, reuse, recycle!***

See page 64 for the words.

'This is Visionscape,' said Steve. 'Our new village for the future. We're going to live there next year because there's a lot of pollution in the city.'

1 Can you see the windows on the roofs?' asked Steve. 'They're solar panels. They're going to give us hot water.'

2 'Can you see the plants in the lake?' asked Anne. 'They're called 'reeds'. They're going to clean the dirty water from the houses.'

3 'Those big boxes at the bottom of the houses are rainwater tanks. They're going to collect all the rainwater,' explained Steve.

4 'Can you see the three wind generators?' asked Anne. 'They move in the wind and they're going to give us electricity.'

5 'Look,' said Anne, 'we're going to grow all our vegetables.'

6 'These green bins are the compost bins,' said Steve. 'We're going to put apple and orange peel in there. The compost makes the ground better.'

'I think your village is going to be amazing,' said Nadia.

....

....

....

....

Tell Compo the answers!

Compo: Hello, everyone.
You: *Hello, Compo.*
Compo: So do you know how we can clean the world now?
You: ...
Compo: Brilliant. So what are you going to recycle now?
You: ...
Compo: Good. Anything else?
You: ...
Compo: What should people do with batteries?
You: ...
Compo: I see. And what can you do to make your school cleaner?
You: ...
Compo: Would you like to live in the Visionscape village?
You: ...

5D How Rainbow Snake started the world

1 Read and listen.

1 A long time ago, there wasn't any day or night. There wasn't any water. There weren't any animals or people. They all slept under the ground.

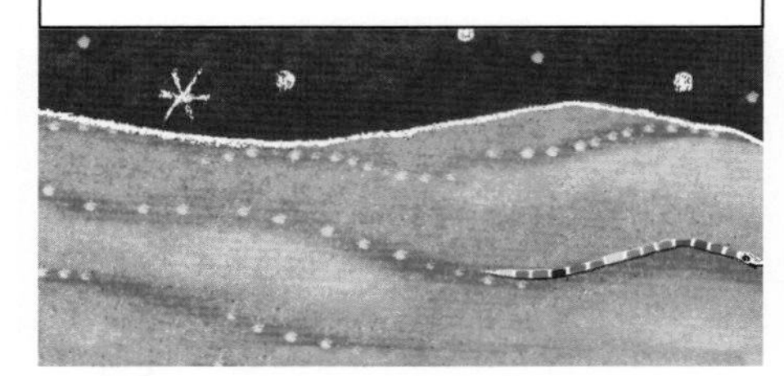

2 One day, Rainbow Snake went to find some friends.

3

4

5

6 Rainbow Snake tickled the frogs' tummies. The frogs laughed and laughed. All the water went up to the ground.

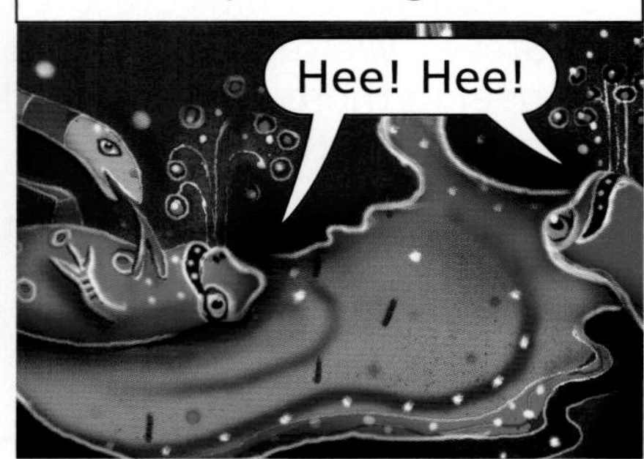

7 The water made rivers and lakes.

8 All the animals came from under the ground. They drank the water in the rivers and lakes.

Project work | Make a story book

2a Fold Cut-out 5.

2b Fold it again twice.

2c Cut along the dotted line.

2d Make your book.

Hold the paper in the middle of the long side with your thumb and first finger.

Push the paper down.

Now you have your book!

3a Listen and write the sentences on the pages.

3b Draw small pictures for the sentences.

Evaluation

4 Which part of the project did you like best?

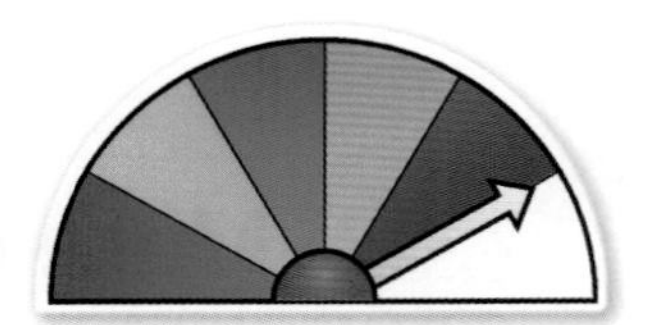

6A How can we help in an accident?

1 Read and listen. What happened to Helen?

1. The children met in the park. 'I liked the village of the future,' said Alex. 'Yes, I think it's better than London a hundred years ago,' said Helen.

2. 'One more question and we can go home,' said Nadia. 'We must ask a question about Science now,' said Alex.

3. Helen sat down. 'Ow! It hurts,' she shouted. 'The glass cut my hand.' There was some blood. 'Oh no, there's nothing in the first aid box,' said Nadia.

4. 'Shall I put this hanky round your hand?' asked Harry. 'Yes, please,' said Helen. 'I know! Shall we ask Compo about first aid?' asked Nadia. 'Yes!' shouted everyone.

5. Harry asked Compo, 'How can we help in an accident?' Compo replied, 'Get your power packs ready and travel!'

6. The children were in the air. Harry shouted, 'Look! We're flying over our school.' 'Hello! Hello!' they shouted but their friends didn't hear them.

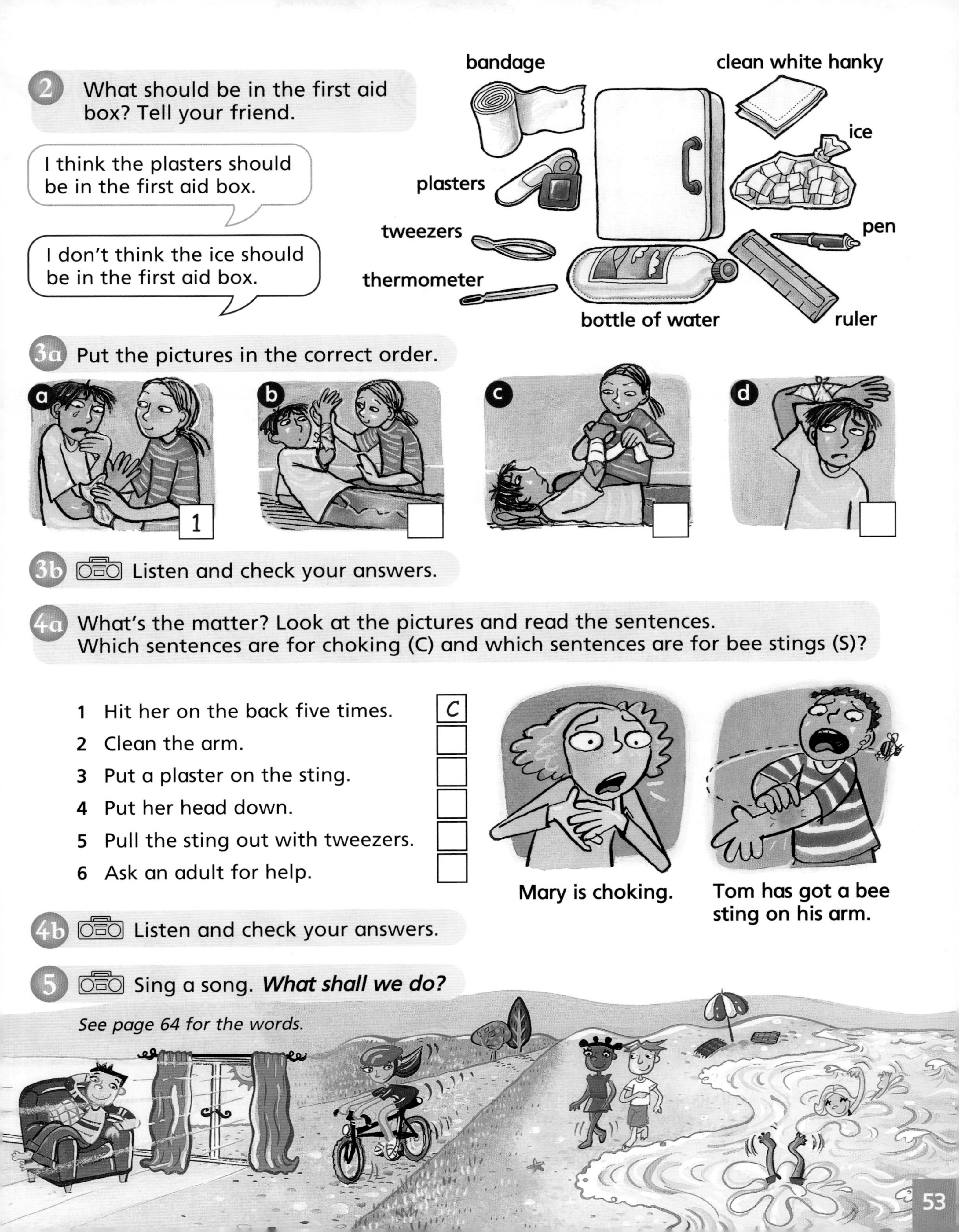

2 What should be in the first aid box? Tell your friend.

I think the plasters should be in the first aid box.

I don't think the ice should be in the first aid box.

3a Put the pictures in the correct order.

3b Listen and check your answers.

4a What's the matter? Look at the pictures and read the sentences. Which sentences are for choking (C) and which sentences are for bee stings (S)?

1 Hit her on the back five times. C
2 Clean the arm.
3 Put a plaster on the sting.
4 Put her head down.
5 Pull the sting out with tweezers.
6 Ask an adult for help.

Mary is choking.

Tom has got a bee sting on his arm.

4b Listen and check your answers.

5 Sing a song. ***What shall we do?***

See page 64 for the words.

6B Home!

1 Read and listen. What did Helen and Harry like doing best?

1. The children came lower and lower. Everyone looked up and saw Harry, Helen, Nadia and Alex. They ran across the playground. 'Hello!' they shouted.

2. The children landed and put their power packs on the ground. Their friends and teacher ran towards them. 'Hello!' they shouted. 'Welcome back!'

3. Everyone had lots of questions. 'Where did you go?' asked Helen's friend, Clare. 'What did you do?' asked Mrs Hudson, the teacher.

4. The children went into the classroom. 'We were lost,' said Harry. 'We answered lots of questions. Then we came home.' 'Yes, and we travelled to different places,' said Nadia.

5. The friends asked questions. 'What did you like best?' they asked. 'I liked drawing everything,' said Helen. 'Yes, and I liked flying with ... the power packs! Where are they?' said Harry.

6. Everyone ran outside. 'Where are the power packs?' asked Harry. Compo said, 'Look up.' They were high in the air. 'They're going to help other children have adventures.'

2 Listen. What do Alex, Nadia, Harry and Helen like doing when they are at home?

1 Harry likes writing emails.

....

2 ....

....

3 ....

....

4 ....

....

5 ....

....

6 ....

....

7 ....

....

8 ....

....

a b c d e f

3 Think. Write some true and false sentences.

Tell your friend. Your friend guesses the true and false sentences.

6C www.cambridge.org/compo

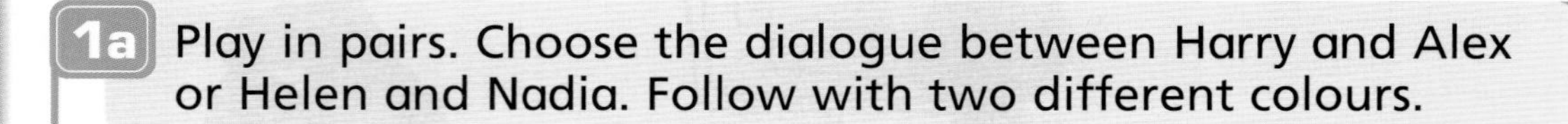

1a Play in pairs. Choose the dialogue between Harry and Alex or Helen and Nadia. Follow with two different colours.

Hi, Helen. Are you awake? 342

About 60. 763

I don't know. Shall we go to the cinema? 768

Yes, There's a new dinosaur film. 737

Yes, thanks. What are you going to do this afternoon? 892

OK. See you at the cinema at six o'clock. Bye! 285

That's a lot! 939

I'm fine. What shall we do today? 365

Yes, I slept for 12 hours! 200

Oh yes! How many have you got? 882

Is your hand better? 345

Hi Alex. How are you? 347

1b Add the numbers in each dialogue. How many kilometres did the children travel? .... km

2 Sing a song. ***Home again!***

See page 64 for the words.

Great! See you at your house about five. Bye! 550

No! No more dinosaurs! 640

Do you want to look at the photos? 588

There's one of the yeti's footprint! 409

Let's see the new Harry Potter film. 634

1c Listen and check your answers.

Tell Compo the answers!

Compo: Hello, everyone.
You: Hello, Compo.
Compo: So are you happy to be home?
You: ...
Compo: I'm pleased. Do you know some first aid now?
You: ...
Compo: Can you tell me what to do for a bee sting?
You: ...
Compo: I see. And what do you do when someone has a bad cut?
You: ...
Compo: Excellent! Did you enjoy finding out about the six questions?
You: ...
Compo: I'm going to help other children now. Goodbye!
You: ...

6D A day in an English school

1 Look at the pictures of a school in England. What is the same at your school? What is different?

2a Work with a friend. Choose three photos each and read the texts.

1 Ruby is nine years old and her brother, Jack, is ten years old. They live in London, England. For school they wear a red and grey uniform. They don't like it: they want to wear comfortable clothes.

2 Every morning all the pupils and teachers go to the big hall for assembly. They sing songs and listen to the headteacher. She tells them about important things for the day. Ruby and Jack don't like sitting on the floor.

3 Then they go to their classrooms. Jack is finishing a History project with his friends today. He likes doing project work but he doesn't like studying History.

4 Then it's break time and all the pupils play in the playground. Ruby and her friends like skipping. It's fun.

5 At lunch time, all the children go to the school dining room for 'school dinners'. The dinner ladies give them their food. Ruby and Jack often have meat pie. They don't like eating school dinners: they want to have pasta.

6 School finishes at 3.30 and they go home in the car. When they get home, they do their homework. Ruby and Jack don't like doing their homework at home: they want to stay at school and use the library and computers in the classroom.

2b Make three questions about your friend's photos. Ask your friend.

How old is Ruby?

2c Listen to the sounds. Where are Ruby and Jack? Write the number.

A in the car ☐
B in the classroom ☐
C in the playground ☐
D in the dining room ☐

Project work A map of your school

3a Choose one floor of your school. Draw a map. Name the places.

3b Choose one place. Cut a piece of paper the same size as the place on your map.

3c Write about what you do there.

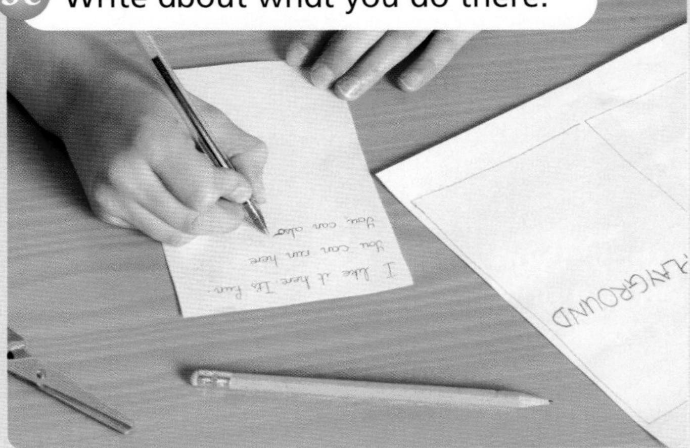

3d Your friend guesses which place it is.

Evaluation

4 What was the most difficult part of the project? What was the easiest?

Revision

1 Play a revision game! Answer the questions, get the power pack and go home!

How to play the game

1 Play in threes. You need dice and counters.

2 Choose two units.
Units 1 and 6
Units 2 and 4
Units 3 and 5

3 Write two questions about your units.
Put them on the table.

4 The first person to get to the power packs answers one of the questions on the table.

5 If you get it right, take the power pack and go home! Zooooom!

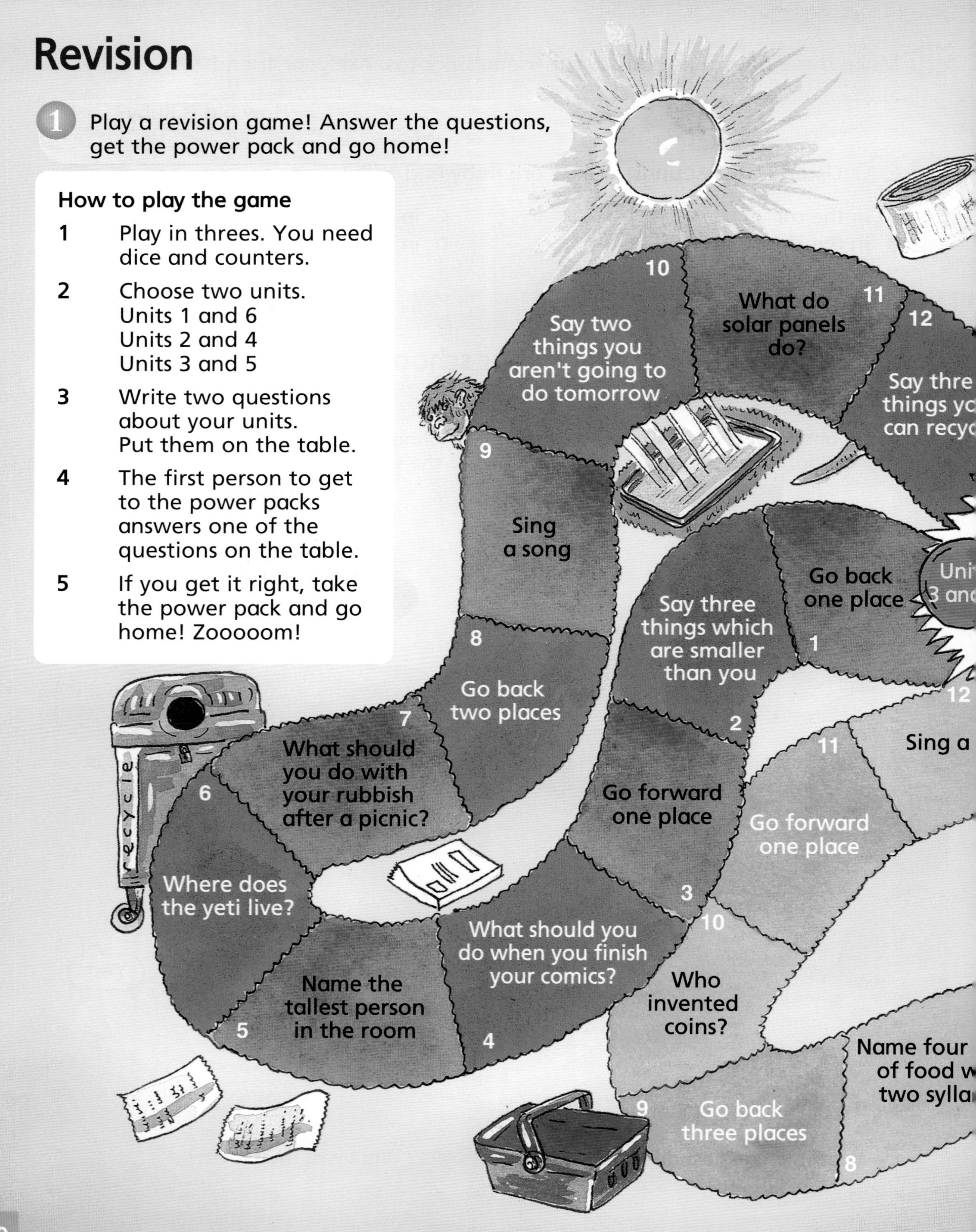

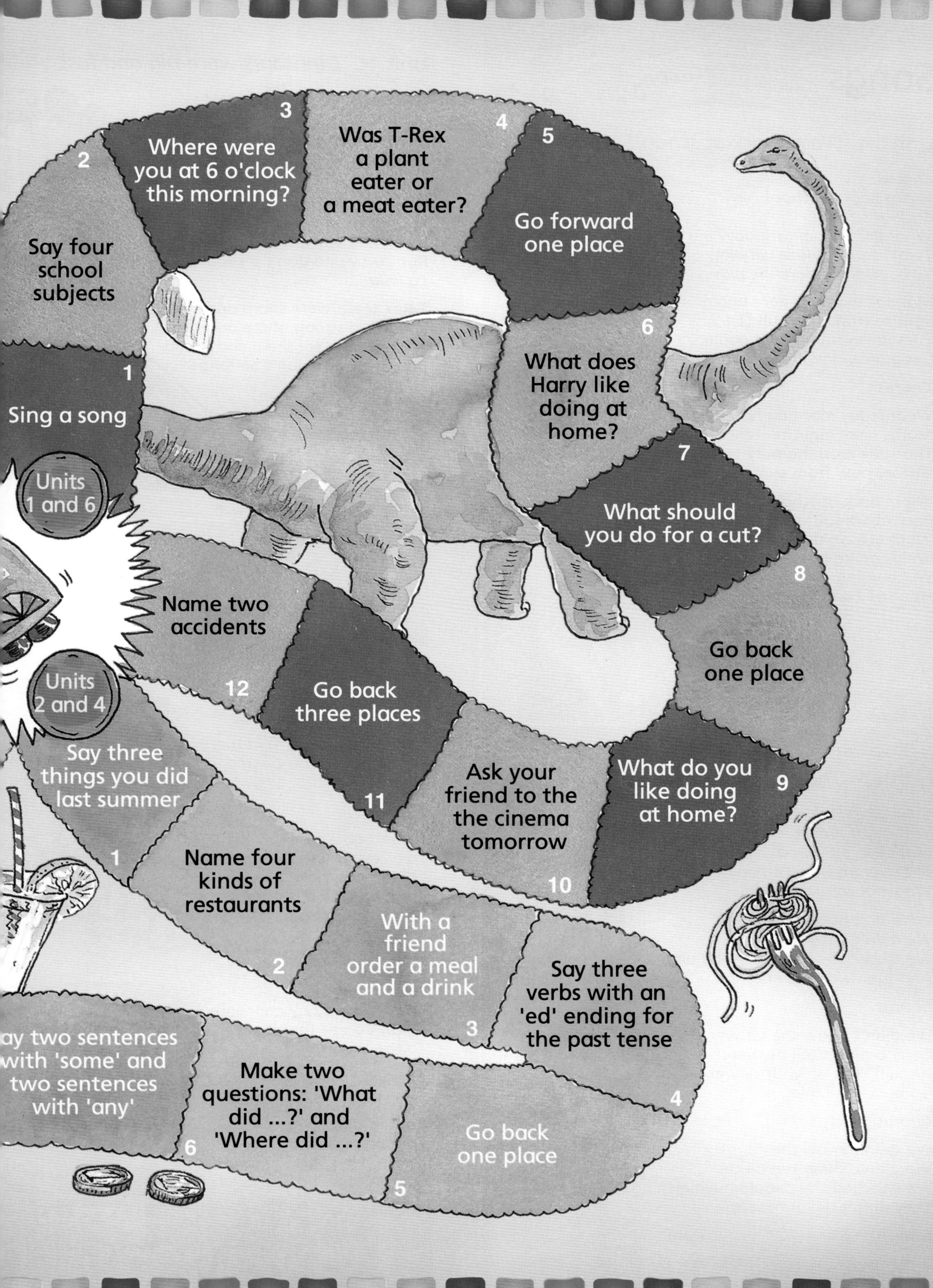
3
Where were you at 6 o'clock this morning?
4
Was T-Rex a plant eater or a meat eater?
5
Go forward one place
2
Say four school subjects
1
Sing a song
6
What does Harry like doing at home?
7
What should you do for a cut?
8
Go back one place
9
What do you like doing at home?
10
Ask your friend to the the cinema tomorrow
11
Go back three places
12
Name two accidents
Units 1 and 6
Units 2 and 4
Say three things you did last summer
1
Name four kinds of restaurants
2
With a friend order a meal and a drink
3
Say three verbs with an 'ed' ending for the past tense
4
Go back one place
5
Make two questions: 'What did ...?' and 'Where did ...?'
6
ay two sentences with 'some' and two sentences with 'any'

Songs

Unit 1A *We're back at school!*

Chorus
We're back at school,
Back at school!
What are we doing today?
Two lessons before we play,
Two lessons before we play.

Monday morning here again,
Science from eight till ten.
Tuesday morning here again,
Geography now from eight till ten.

Chorus

Wednesday morning here again,
Maths from eight till ten.
Thursday morning here again,
History now from eight till ten.

We're back at school,
Back at school!
What are we doing today?
We're going home!
We're going out to play today, hooray!
Hooray! Today we play!

Unit 2A *The money song*

Chorus
We've got money in our pockets,
Money in our hand.
But who invented money?
We want to understand.

We didn't have a question,
We didn't know where to go.
We tossed the coin up in the air,
And then we asked Compo.

Chorus

We didn't know the answer,
Compo didn't tell us then.
He said, 'Put on your power packs.
Go back in time again.'

Chorus

We didn't know the country,
We didn't know the places.
We watched the people buying things,
They didn't see our faces.

Chorus

Unit 1C *Dinosaurs were big and fast*

Dinosaurs were big and fast,
Big and fast, big and fast,
Dinosaurs were big and fast,
Run away and don't be last!
La la la …

T Rex feet were very wide,
Very wide, very wide,
T Rex feet were very wide,
Run away and don't try to hide!
La la la …

T Rex teeth were sharp and strong,
Sharp and strong, sharp and strong,
T Rex teeth were sharp and strong,
Run away and don't be long!
La la la …

Unit 2C *Where did you go last night?*

Chorus
Where did you go, where did you go,
Where did you go?
Where did you go, where did you go,
Last night?

I didn't go
To the cinema,
I didn't see a new film there.
I didn't go to the cinema,
To the cinema.

Chorus

I didn't go
To a restaurant,
I didn't eat a big meal there.
I didn't go to a restaurant,
To a restaurant.

Chorus

I didn't go
To the theatre,
I didn't see a big star there.
I didn't go to the theatre,
To the theatre.

Chorus

I went, we went
Back in time
To see the old coins there.
I went, we went
Back in time, back in time.

Chorus

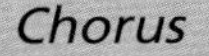

Unit 3A *The syllable song*

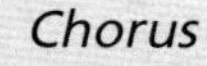

Chorus
How many syllables?
Count with me.
How many syllables?
One, two, three.
How many syllables?
Count with me,
One, two, three.

One for day
And one for night,
One for dark
And one for light,
One for wrong
And one for right.

Chorus

Two for mountain
And two for power,
Two for minute
And two for hour,
Two for sunshine
And two for flower.

Chorus

Three for important
And banana,
Three for exciting
And delicious,
Three for amazing
Dinosaur!

Chorus

Unit 3C *Monsters! Monsters! Monsters!*

Monsters! Monsters! Monsters!
There are monsters everywhere.
Monsters! Monsters! Monsters!
Green and red with long black hair.
Aaargh!

Are there monsters in the mountains?
Are there monsters in the sea?
Are there monsters in the desert?
And are they watching me?
No!

Are there monsters up above us?
Are there monsters in that tree?
Are there monsters in my bedroom?
And are they looking at me?
No!

Are there monsters in my garden?
Are there monsters in the park?
Are there monsters in the bathroom?
And are they looking for me?
No!

Monsters! Monsters! Monsters!
There are monsters everywhere.
Monsters! Monsters! Monsters!
Green and red with long black hair,
Green and red with long black hair!

Unit 4A *The picnic song*

Chorus
Today's the day
We're waiting for,
Today's the day
For our picnic!
Today's the day
We're waiting for
Our P I C N I C picnic!

We can have some P P P for pizza
And some I I I for ice cream,
But we haven't got any cake!

Chorus

We can have some P P P for pizza
And some I I I for ice cream,
But we haven't got any crisps!

Chorus

Unit 4C *Food, food, wonderful food!*

Food, food, wonderful food!
Food, food, wonderful food!
Food in the morning ...
Please make us some food
And we'll eat it all the time!

Food for breakfast, ...
Pam, pass the jam.
Fred, pass the bread.
And thank you, thank you,
Thank you!

Food, food, wonderful food!
Food, food, wonderful food!
Food at lunchtime, ...
Please make us some food
And we'll eat it all the time!

Food for lunch, ...
Pete, pass the meat.
Please, pass the peas.
And thank you, thank you,
Thank you!

Food, food, wonderful food!
Food, food, wonderful food!
Food in the evening, ...
Please make us some food
And we'll eat it all the time!

Food for dinner, ...
Walt, pass the salt.
Bruce, pass the juice.
And thank you, thank you,
Thank you!

Food, food, wonderful food!
Food, food, wonderful food!
Food in the morning,
Food in the evening,
Please make us some food
And we'll eat it all the time,
All the time!
Please make us some food
And we'll eat it all the time!

Unit 5A *Rubbish! Rubbish! Rubbish!*

Rubbish! (Rubbish!)
There's a lot of it about.
Think very carefully,
Before you throw it out.
...

Chorus
All around the world.
(Rubbish! Rubbish!)
All around the world.
(Rubbish! Rubbish!)

All around the world.
(Rubbish! Rubbish!)
All around the world.
(Rubbish! Rubbish!)
Rubbish!

Rubbish! (Rubbish!)
There's a lot of it around.
Think very carefully,
Don't throw it on the ground.
...

Chorus

Rubbish! (Rubbish!)
There's a lot from you and me.
Think very carefully,
Don't throw it in the sea.
...

Unit 5C *Reduce, reuse, recycle!*

Chorus
Reduce, reuse, recycle!
Let's see what we can do.
Reduce, reuse, recycle!
And let's see what we can do.

When you finish a bottle,
Don't throw it in the bins.
Let's take it for recycling,
And do the same with tins.

Chorus

When you finish with paper,
Don't throw it right away.
Let's take it for recycling,
We can do that every day.

Chorus

When you finish your batteries,
Don't throw them in the street.
Let's take them for recycling,
And keep the city neat!

Chorus

Unit 6A *What shall we do?*

Chorus
What shall we do with this lovely day,
What shall we do with this lovely day,
What shall we do with this lovely day,
So early in the morning?

Shall we go for a walk along the beach
Or stay at home all day?
Shall we go for a walk along the beach
Or stay at home all day?

Chorus

Shall we go for a bike ride in the country
Or stay at home all day?
Shall we go for a bike ride in the country
Or stay at home all day?

Chorus

Shall we go for a swim in the clear blue water
Or stay at home all day?
Shall we go for a swim in the clear blue water
Or stay at home all day?

Chorus

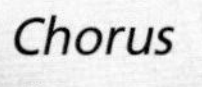

Unit 6C *Home again!*

Chorus
Home again, home again,
Home again, home!
Let's say 'Hello!' and say,
'We're back today!'

'Where did you go?
What did you see?'
We'll answer your questions,
One, two, three.

Chorus

'What did you eat?
What did you draw?'
We'll answer your questions,
Two, three, four.

Chorus

'Where did you sleep?
What did you drink?'
We'll answer your questions,
Just let us think.

Chorus